THE ESSENTIAL EXERCISE

and

BIRTHBALL HANDBOOK

for

Pregnancy and Beyond

by

MARK HIBBITTS

&

MARTIN BECKLEY

Miracle Products Ltd

Published by

Miracle Products Ltd.

PO BOX 1205

Beaconsfield

Bucks HP9 2GQ

customerservice@themiraclebox.co.uk

Printed and bound in Great Britain by
CPI Antony Rowe, Chippenham, Wiltshire

ISBN
978-0-9560134-0-8

Contents

About the Authors

Mark Hibbitts

Mark is well known within the fitness industry as the founder of Newborn Fitness. A qualified personal fitness coach and a full member of The Guild of Pregnancy & Postnatal Exercise teachers, Mark is resident Pregnancy Fitness Expert for lifestylexperts.com and supernanny.co.uk. He writes regularly for Women's Fitness Magazine.

Martin Beckley

Martin is a successful entrepreneur, with a string of health, fitness and lifestyle businesses. Martin is also a personal trainer and founder of the Miracle Box, the UK's best selling complete birthing/exercise ball package for mums and mums to be.

Forward

One day in summer 2007, with the sun shining and the barbeque blazing, Michelle Hibbitts and Denise Beckley were talking about children. As both wives were in their mid 30's with one year old babies, the conversation soon moved round to the difficulty of getting back in shape after the birth. It turned out that both ladies had used a birth-ball during pregnancy and labour, and also (perhaps not surprisingly with personal trainer husbands) to regain their figures afterwards. *'Well it's ok for us'* said Denise, *'we know what to do, but what about all the mums who use their ball during labour and then never use it again? Can't you two do something to help them?'* Well the answer was definitely *'Yes, we could'*, and the idea for **The Essential Exercise and Birth ball Handbook for Pregnancy and Beyond** was born.

Apart from getting full use from your exercise/birth-ball, the aim of the handbook is to give you important advice and instruction to keep you fitter during pregnancy, help you through the birthing process, and enable you to enjoy a faster recovery. With our fitness industry backgrounds we realised that many 'exercise books' read like scientific manuals, so we've set out to make this handbook as straightforward and easy to understand as possible. You'll learn when you can and cannot exercise, the benefits you'll receive from exercise, and how you should exercise safely. You'll then be taken through safe and effective pregnancy, postnatal, and advanced exercise ball routines.

One of our main goals was to make this book exceptional value for money, so we've added our *'8 Super Secrets for getting your pre-pregnancy figure back FAST'* and finally, as an extra bonus, we've included our previously unreleased DVD *'A Simple Guide to Pelvic Floor and Core Exercises'*.

We hope you enjoy the book and the DVD, and we wish you all the very best for your pregnancy.......and beyond!

Mark Hibbitts and Martin Beckley

Disclaimer

Any exercise carries with it an element of risk. Your doctor or health care provider should be consulted before commencing an exercise or nutritional programme, especially during pregnancy or the postnatal period. The exercises in this book are recommendations only and are not designed to constitute a full exercise programme. All exercises are performed at your own risk. If you feel pain or discomfort during exercise you should stop immediately.

This book is for educational purposes only and any advice therein is not a substitute for medical advice from your own doctor or health care provider. The authors and publisher specifically disclaim any and all liability arising directly or indirectly from the use or application of any information contained in this book. Always consult your doctor or health care provider regarding your specific situation, or if you are in any way concerned about your health.

If you are unsure of any exercise please consult with a qualified fitness professional before commencing. Qualified and insured trainers can be found at **www.newbornfitness.co.uk** & **www.lifestylexperts.com**

1

Introduction

The benefits of exercise/birth balls are now well known. Due to the recommendation of midwives everywhere they are fast becoming an essential part of every mum-to-be's labour kit. Unfortunately, most mums are unsure what to do with their ball other than sit on it, and it's a shame that something that could be their route to an easier pregnancy, shorter labour, and faster return to their pre-pregnancy muscle tone, gets used incorrectly, and then thrown away or left to rot in the loft or garage. This book solves that problem by teaching you not only the benefits of using a ball, but showing you in clear and easy to understand terms, exactly how it should be done.

What the professionals say about birth balls:

"I recommend birth balls to all my clients. They are great ante-natally to aid posture and balance as well as being ideal to use during exercise. During labour they can be used in several ways as a means of support and to open the pelvis up to its widest diameter. I carry one for myself as a midwife in labour to sit on to ease my tired back!"

Vicky Feeney. Midwife.

www.liverpoolindependentmidwives.co.uk

"I encourage all my mums to use a birth ball. It really helps to keep them active during labour"

Laura Davies. Doula.

www.babyonboarddoulas.co.uk

"I would always introduce the exercise/birth ball into my sessions as it provides postural relief for the pre and post natal ladies whilst providing a challenging workout safely. The pre and post natal market especially have come to expect the ball in workouts and therefore the knowledge for clients of how to get safe and effective use of it is paramount!"

Madeline Carson. Pregnancy & Postnatal Exercise Specialist.

www.fitnessandbeyond.co.uk

"I use the birth ball in all my training with my clients - initially to really start working their core stability and balance and then incorporate it when using weights. Brilliant piece of equipment, so versatile and can be used for all abilities."

Vicki Hill. Vicki Hill Personal Training, Bristol.

"I am a Personal Trainer but also a new mum who gave birth at home recently. I use a ball with all my clients to improve posture and core stability, it is a fun way to work out and everyone is able to progress with this piece of equipment and so gain the added satisfaction that they can both feel the results physically and see what they have achieved over a period of time. I also find some of my smaller groups laugh a lot when using the ball especially when facing a new challenge! I used my ball during labour (which was

Introduction

very quick) both to lean and sit on and it made a big difference - I also think they bring some comfort to the labouring mum as they are soft and easy to use. I don't think I would ever not use a ball with a client and always use them in my circuit training classes. A must for pre/post natal exercise and great during labour."

Lisa Moore. Personal Trainer & Mother.

"I am both a qualified personal trainer and a Mum, My youngest Son is 10 Months old and my eldest is 2. I trained in the gym throughout both my pregnancies and the ball played a significant part in my training. I used it instead of a bench when doing weights and used it against the wall to support me whilst doing squats and lunges. I even used it at work to sit on rather than a chair. I have always used it to train other people and have used it myself with great success to get back my pre pregnancy shape. During my pregnancy I used to lay across it all the time to take the pressure off my back and during labour I wouldn't have been without it. The ball is such a diverse piece of equipment with countless benefits. My son likes playing with it too!"

Karen Heslop. Personal Trainer & Mother.

2

The Benefits of Exercise during Pregnancy

It's true that exercise during pregnancy has tremendous benefits for the mum to be. Dr James Clapp, probably the most well known and respected researcher in the field of pre and post natal fitness, states that "women who perform activity for 45 minute sessions at least 5 times per week will get the most benefit from exercise during pregnancy"

The benefits for mum can include:

Less risk of gestational diabetes

Less risk of pregnancy induced hypertension

Fewer obstetric interventions (forceps, venteuse)

Reduction in active labour time

Possible reduction in c-section deliveries

Increased maternal wellbeing

A quicker return to pre-pregnancy figure

More pre & postnatal bladder control

Reduction in leg cramps, back pain, etc.

Less bone density loss during lactation

As if that's not enough, it's great for baby too!

The benefits for baby can include:

Less body fat at birth (which can possibly extend into later life)

Infants can be less cranky, with reduced colic

Greater neuro-developmental scores in oral language and motor skill at age 5

So you can see for yourself how exercise can have a very positive effect on your pregnancy. However there are several contra-indications to pregnancy exercise so it's very important that you consult with your doctor or midwife before commencing any type of pregnancy exercise program.

Ref: Nordahl Petersen Jeffreys, Fit to Deliver 2005

3

Pregnancy Exercise Contra-Indications

Absolute Contra-Indications to pregnancy exercise:

- Significant heart disease
- Restrictive lung disease
- Incompetent cervix
- Multiple gestation with premature labour risk
- Persistent 2nd or 3rd trimester bleeding
- Placenta Previa after 26 weeks
- Current premature labour
- Ruptured membranes
- Preeclampsia/pregnancy induced hypertension

Relative Contra-Indications to pregnancy exercise:

- Severe Anaemia
- Cardiac arrhythmia
- Chronic Bronchitis
- Poorly controlled type 1 diabetes
- Extreme Morbid obesity

- Extreme Underweight (BMI <12)

- Sedentary lifestyle

- Intrauterine growth restriction in current pregnancy

- Poorly controlled hypertension

- Orthopaedic limitations

- Poorly controlled seizure disorder

- Poorly controlled hyperthyroidism

- Heavy Smoker

If none of the contra-indications apply to you then you're ok to start exercising, but you still need to be aware of potential risks. You must stop exercising immediately if you experience:

- Vaginal bleeding

- Dyspnea prior to exertion (Out of Breath, prior to exercise)

- Dizziness

- Headache

- Chest pain

- Muscle weakness

- Calf pain or swelling (DVT must be ruled out)

- Preterm labour

- Decreased fetal movement

- Amniotic fluid leakage

Ref: American College Of Gynaecologists (ACOG) 2002

Exercise during Pregnancy

4

Introduction to Pregnancy Exercise

Top Tip

"You should always warm up thoroughly before exercising, cool down properly afterwards, and finish your workout by performing the stretching exercises listed in this book (refer to Appendix 1). Thoroughly warming up will prevent a sudden rise in blood pressure and reduce the chance of muscle and joint injury. Cooling down properly limits the risk of post exercise hypotension (low blood pressure)"

Firing your 'core'

When you first get your ball we recommend you start by sitting on it until you find your balance and feel completely comfortable before commencing any exercises. The instability of the ball will make your 'core' muscles come into play, and learning to engage those muscles correctly is very important if you are to enjoy the real benefit of these ball exercises.

Your transverse abdominus (TVA) is the innermost abdominal muscle that wraps around your trunk like a corset (highlighted in fig. 1). The ability to contract your TVA will not only flatten your tummy, but also help to maintain good posture, alleviate back pain, and prevent injury. To find your TVA, lie on your back and put your fingertips inside your hip bones. If you cough you'll feel your TVA twitch beneath your fingers. To contract the TVA take a deep breath in, and then breathe out and at the same time pull your belly button in towards your spine. When you've mastered this, try holding the contraction for 10 seconds while continuing to breathe. It will be tricky at first but once you've learned to 'fire and sustain' the TVA you will be able to switch it on any time you exercise, lift baby, or do anything else that requires effort. Although your 'core' also consists of other muscles, contracting one part, (in this case the TVA) will engage the other parts synergistically.

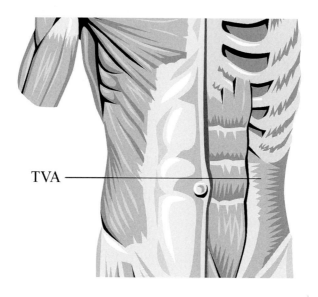

TVA

Fig.1

Now you've decided to start a pregnancy exercise programme, please don't be concerned about athletic prowess. During pregnancy your goal should be to maintain your fitness levels rather than increase them. However, as your core muscles get used to exercise they will become stronger and the exercises will become easier. As a rule of thumb you can increase your stability on the ball at the start by performing exercises with your feet wider apart. This makes the exercises easier to perform. As you become stronger and more confident you can increase the difficulty of the exercise by decreasing the distance between your feet.

As your pregnancy progresses the hormone relaxin will be present in your body. This will soften your connective tissue to prepare your body for the birth, so it's important you don't over-extend your joints and only stretch to the biting point (where you start to feel the stretch). Going beyond that could possibly result in serious injury. After your first trimester it is advisable not to lie on your back for more than 30 seconds. Usually this problem can be solved by performing your exercises on a slight incline.

Don't bother wearing a heart rate monitor during pregnancy as the increase in your blood volume at this time will make the reading inefficient. During pregnancy it is more useful to use the talk-test as an exertion guideline, and if you find it impossible to carry on a conversation while exercising it's time to slow down.

Top Tip

The American College of Obstetricians and Gynaecologists (ACOG 2002) state that *"In the absence of contra-indications pregnant women are encouraged to engage in 30 minutes or more of moderate exercise on most, if not all, days of the week."*

The pregnancy exercises in this book are divided into different body part sections. We suggest that each time you workout you take 2 exercises from each section; **upper body, lower body, waistline,** and **balance**, and perform 2-3 sets of each exercise. Start with the larger movements, and vary the exercises so over a period of time you get the best all round balance and development. Do all the stretches at the end of each workout. A workout like this should be completed within 45 minutes including a warm-up and cool-down.

As you get stronger you'll find some of the exercises will get easier, so your exercise programme will be more beneficial and interesting if regular progressions are made to it. To do this you can:

- Increase the number of repetitions per set
- Increase the resistance/weight used in the exercise
- Decrease the amount of rest between sets
- Perform the repetitions more slowly
- Emphasise the negative (lowering) portion of the exercise

All these are methods of increasing the intensity of the exercises which will in turn lead to better muscle tone, increased fat loss, and greater strength. They also make your workouts more enjoyable as you'll be able to measure your progress, and nothing is more motivating than seeing continuous improvement.

Remember:

- For increased stability keep your feet wide apart
- Warm-Up and Cool-Down thoroughly
- Choose 2 exercises from each section & vary each time for all round development
- Perform all the stretches at the end of each workout (refer to Appendix 1)

Introduction to Pregnancy Exercise

- Stretch only to 'biting point'
- Don't lay 'on your back' for more than 30 seconds after the first trimester
- Increase the intensity for continued improvement
- If you experience pain or discomfort stop immediately

5

Your Pregnancy Ball Routine

Quick Start Guide

This quick start guide is provided as a reminder for those of you who have read the book, checked with your health care provider, received the go ahead, and are ready to get started. Please do not start using this guide unless you have read and understood the exercise guidelines and contra-indications mentioned previously, and have been given the all clear to exercise. Doing so could be dangerous for you and your baby.

- Make sure you are wearing appropriate clothing and have your water ready
- Choose the two exercises for upper body, lower body, waistline, and balance that you wish to perform today
- Turn on your music and begin your warm up.
- Exercise!
- Cool down and don't forget to stretch (refer to Appendix 1)
- Well done! It's time to relax until your next workout.

Important stuff!

- If you feel unstable, place your feet wider apart
- Repeat each exercise 2-3 times
- Stretch only to 'biting point' and not beyond
- Increase the intensity for continued improvement
- Don't lie on your back for too long after the first trimester
- Keep hydrated
- If it hurts, stop right away

Incline Flyes... for improved chest tone
- Upper Body Pregnancy Exercises

1. Holding two hand weights sit on the ball and roll out until your upper back is resting on the ball
2. Drop your hips until you are in an incline position, contract TVA and hold the weights up above your eyes
3. With elbows bent, lower the weights out to your side until a very slight stretch is felt in your chest muscles
4. In the same arc, return to the start position
5. Perform 12-15 repetitions. Be careful not to overstretch

Incline Dumbell Press... for upper chest toning
- Upper Body Pregnancy Exercises

1. Holding two hand weights sit on the ball and roll out until your upper back is resting on the ball
2. Drop your hips until you are in an incline position, contract TVA and press the weights up above your eyes
3. Lower the weights until your elbows are at a 90 degree angle
4. Push back to the start position, and repeat 12-15 times

Press Up on Ball... for toned arms and chest
- Upper Body Pregnancy Exercises

1. Kneel in front of the ball and place hands on ball at arms length, contract TVA
2. Keeping your back straight bend elbows until your elbows are at 90 degrees
3. Pause, then return to the start position
4. Repeat 12-15 times. If the ball rolls away place it against a wall

Your Pregnancy Ball Routine

Bicep Curls... to strengthen and tone your upper arms - Upper Body Pregnancy Exercises (a must to help with lifting your baby)

1. Sit upright on the ball, contract TVA
2. Hold hand weights at arms length, contract TVA
3. Keeping elbows pointing down curl weights to shoulders
4. Lower and repeat 12-15 times

Dyna-Band Curls… to strengthen your upper arms - Upper Body Pregnancy Exercises

1. Sit upright on ball, place dyna-bands under feet
2. Hold handles at arms length, contract TVA
3. Keeping elbows pointing down curl bands to shoulders
4. Lower and repeat 12-15 times

Tricep Extensions... tone the back of your arms
- Upper Body Pregnancy Exercises

1. Holding two hand weights sit on the ball and roll out until your upper back is resting on the ball
2. Drop your hips until you are in an incline position, contract TVA and push the weights up above your eyes
3. Keeping your elbows pointed upwards, lower the weights slowly to your forehead, do not touch though!
4. Return to start position and repeat 12-15 times

Your Pregnancy Ball Routine

Lateral Raises... tone your shoulders
- Upper Body Pregnancy Exercises

1. Sit on the ball with arms at your sides, contract TVA
2. Keeping your arms slightly bent raise your arms to just below shoulder height
3. Return to the start position and repeat 12 -15 times
4. To increase resistance use hand weights or dyna-bands

Squat... great for toned thighs and bottom
- Lower Body Pregnancy Exercises

1. Stand with your feet shoulder width apart
2. Place ball between the curve of your back and the wall, contract TVA
3. Bend your knees, squat down to 90 degrees and return to start position
4. Repeat 12-15 times

Split Squats... tone your thighs and bottom
- Lower Body Pregnancy Exercises

1. Stand with feet together and ball between the curve of your back and the wall
2. Contract your TVA, then keeping head up and back straight step forward into a split position
3. Bend until your front thigh is parallel to the floor, not letting your front knee pass your toes
4. Return to start position and repeat 12-15 times on each leg

Your Pregnancy Ball Routine

Calf Raises... tone your calves
- Lower Body Pregnancy Exercises

1. Sit on the ball and place your feet a few inches apart
2. Contract TVA, raise heels off floor and contract your calf muscles
3. Hold for a count of 3 and return to start position
4. Repeat 12-15 times

Pelvic Tilts… for core and abdominals

- Waistline Pregnancy Exercises

1. Sit upright on the ball
2. Contract your TVA
3. Without moving your feet tilt your pelvis forward and upward
4. Hold for 5 seconds and return to start position
5. Repeat 12-15 times

Sit Backs… working your core and abdominals
- Waistline Pregnancy Exercises

1. Sit on the front half of the ball keeping knees bent and feet flat on floor
2. Cross your arms on your chest and contract your TVA
3. Slowly lean back 30-40 degrees letting the ball roll to support your lower back
4. Return to starting position and repeat 10-15 times

Lateral Pelvic Tilt... for core and abdominals

- Waistline Pregnancy Exercises

1. Sit on ball with hands on hips and feet on floor. Contract TVA
2. Keeping head shoulders and feet in place slowly tilt your pelvis to the left
3. Hold the position for a few seconds and return to the start position
4. Perform 12-15 times then repeat on other side

Seated Balance...great balance exercise
- Waistline Pregnancy Exercises

1. Sit upright on ball with hands on the ball for stability
2. Contract TVA, then keeping your back straight raise one foot 8-12 inches off the floor
3. Hold the position for a few seconds then return to the start position
4. Aim to repeat 10 times

Ball Twists... work your core, obliques and balance - Waistline Pregnancy Exercises

1. Sit on ball with knees bent and feet flat on floor
2. Contract TVA and lean back 20-30 degrees
3. Hold a ball or small dumbbell in front with arms straight
4. Slowly rotate your upper body from side to side 12-15 times, try not to move your hips

Standing Balance... great for balance and core muscles - Waistline Pregnancy Exercises

1. Stand upright with your feet a few inches apart
2. Place the ball between the curve of your back and the wall
3. Contract TVA then slowly raise one leg about 12 inches from the floor
4. Hold for a few seconds then return to starting position
5. Repeat 12 times then repeat on the other leg

Advanced Balance... core muscles
- Waistline Pregnancy Exercises

1. Sit upright with hands on ball for stability
2. Contract TVA, then keeping good posture raise you arms out to your sides and one foot off the floor 8-12 inches
3. Hold for a few seconds and return to start position
4. Aim for 10 repetitions. This should only be performed by advanced exercisers

Your Pregnancy Ball Routine

Hip Flexor Stretch

- Stretching Pregnancy Exercises

1. Sit on the ball
2. Slide one leg behind ball until straight
3. Maintaining your balance lean back slightly until a stretch is felt at the top of your thigh
4. Hold for 15 seconds and repeat on other side
5. If balance is an issue hold on to a wall or table

Hamstring Stretch

- Stretching Pregnancy Exercises

1. Sit on the ball with legs bent and feet flat on floor
2. Place hands on thighs and lean slightly forward
3. Keeping chest up and back straight slowly straighten your legs
4. Hold for 15 seconds and return to start position

Upper Back Stretch
- Stretching Pregnancy Exercises

1. Kneel in front of the ball
2. Roll the ball away from your body
3. With head between your arms lean forward until you feel the stretch in your chest back and shoulders
4. Hold for 15 seconds and return to the start position

Your Pregnancy Ball Routine

Chest Stretch
- Stretching Pregnancy Exercises

1. Kneel on the floor with the ball at your side
2. Bend at the waist and roll the ball out to arms length
3. Lean forward slightly until a stretch is felt in your chest
4. Hold for 15 seconds and return to start position

Cat Stretch
- Stretching Pregnancy Exercises

1. Kneel down on the floor with your arms out in front of you
2. Lower your head and push hands into the floor and body upwards, whilst arching your back like a cat
3. Hold for 15 seconds and release

Calf Stretch

- Stretching Pregnancy Exercises

1. Lean forward against a wall or pole with your right leg out behind you
2. Slowly lower your right heel to the ground and at the same time push your hips towards the wall
3. When you feel a stretch in the calf hold for 15 seconds
4. Repeat on the other side

6

Labour, Birth and Your Ball

"I used the ball in the early stages of my labour. After about 45mins I said I thought I might need the Tens machine only to be told I had been using the ball for over 2hrs. It definitely helped me with the time whilst in labour"

Michelle Watson, new mum.

A Midwifes Perspective

The birth ball is a simple yet amazing piece of essential kit for any pregnant woman. It can be used before and after birth for fitness as well being an excellent birth aid.

In its most basic form a woman can simply sit on a birth ball and instantly improve her posture, ease back pain, and relax, as well as using it to exercise her pelvic floor muscles, and this can be done with very little instruction. Also, when one sits on a birth ball, the legs naturally drop to the sides, thus opening the pelvis to its widest diameter and aiding optimal fetal positioning in preparation for labour.

In labour, a woman should be encouraged to take up positions naturally and a birth ball can assist her into positions to support her weight and help her to relax. Upright positions are more favourable for labour as recumbent positions can make contractions more painful, so using a birth ball to stay upright will not only help a woman deal with contractions more effectively, but may even shorten the length of labour. Rocking on the ball, aids descent and rotation of the baby into the pelvis and doing this during contractions can give the labouring woman another means of focus.

Postnatally, the birth ball can be used to strengthen pelvic floor muscles which is an essential exercise following birth. It can also be used to strengthen the hips, buttocks and thighs whilst aiding posture which can be affected after pregnancy. Bouncing on the ball with baby can help soothe a fretful child which is better than walking the floor rocking a crying baby!

I recommend the birth ball to all of my pregnant ladies and just about all of them have used it in labour and have found it invaluable

Vicky Feeney - Midwife

www.liverpoolindependentmidwives.co.uk

Labour, Birth, and Your Ball

The 'Non-Exercise' Benefits of Birth Balls during Pregnancy and Labour

If you're pregnant and you have any doubts about whether a ball would be good for you, just sit on one and it should erase any concerns pretty quickly! It always amuses us to see the look on a heavily pregnant woman's face when she sits on a ball for the first time. The relief is a joy to behold as the pressure is taken off her weary back muscles, and she finds herself sitting comfortably, often for the first time in a long while.

But there's actually a lot more to 'birth balls' than finding a comfortable place to sit. Because a ball creates an unstable base to sit on compared to a chair, your core muscles (those that form a corset around your body and support your spine) are involuntarily brought into action to keep you balanced. This forces you to use good posture, builds your core strength, and alleviates a lot of the back pain associated with late pregnancy.

However, the number one reason why midwives recommend birth balls to their mums is because of what they call 'optimal foetal position'. This is a theory developed by a midwife, Jean Sutton, and Pauline Scott, an antenatal teacher, who found that the mother's position and movement could influence the way her baby lay in the womb in the final weeks of pregnancy. Many difficult labours result from 'mal-presentation', where the baby's position makes it hard for the head to move through the pelvis, so changing the way the baby lies could make birth easier for mother and child.

Lounging around on the settee in front of the TV each evening as many of us tend to do these days, is a major cause of baby getting **'back to back'**, and your ball will be great for helping with this. It will provide a firm yet comfortable place to sit, and swaying your hips around in a circle or side to side during late pregnancy and labour can encourage baby to turn. It's also very good for your core and pelvic muscles and to help you relax.

Top Tip

"Leaning over your ball can also be very comfortable and will help to stretch out your tired back muscles. It also provides a great position for your partner or Doula to give you a back rub, or apply counter pressure".

What the mums say:

"I used a ball at some point or other with all of my 3 pregnancies/births. I hired one for my first baby – I used it every day in the month up to having my little girl and found it really eased labour pains. In fact, my first labour was only about five hours long and I'm sure it helped. I bobbed up and down on the ball with my final baby to help break the waters which didn't want to break on their own. The birth came on really quickly and I would thoroughly recommend them to other soon-to-be-mums – if it's only to take your mind off the pains!!"

Helen Murphy, New Mum.

"The birth ball is the only thing I can get comfortable on at 38 weeks pregnant! It's helped with back problems and posture and I'm hoping it will also help make things more comfortable when I go into labour. I will definitely be using it afterwards to help regain my figure"

Sarah Wyatt, New Mum.

"As someone who had done fitness workouts on the birth ball prior to falling pregnant I had no idea how useful it would be while I was pregnant. I have 8 weeks to go and I find it invaluable as I can't get comfy on normal chairs or sofas sometimes. I also use it for stretching and doing pelvic floor exercises. After my antenatal class I also know I will be using it throughout labour as well."

Andrea Vick, New Mum.

"During the last few months of pregnancy I developed SPD (Symphasis Pubis Dysfunction) which was extremely painful and I found it difficult to walk, turn over in bed and even sit down. The only place I could sit comfortably was on the birthing ball as it helped to support the muscles that were affected by the SPD, and also helped the baby to get into position during labour when again it was the only place I found most comfortable to sit, in between contractions. I believe that sitting on the ball during labour helped me to dilate a lot faster than if I hadn't been sitting on it."

Kate Whorlow, New Mum.

www.angelchakra.co.uk

"My birth ball has been invaluable. I have suffered with SPD during this pregnancy but the ball has really helped alleviate the pain and discomfort I have felt. I use my ball most nights as a chair - much to everyone's amusement! - I find it relaxes my pelvic area as well as taking the weight off my pubic bones. I also do a couple of exercises with the birthball:

1. I sit on the ball and rock gently form side to side, sometimes making a figure of eight

2. I lay across the birth ball (supine) and give myself a full back stretch
It's been a godsend!"

Cass Bergin, New Mum.

"I used my birth ball during pregnancy and all the way through my labour. It was comfortable to sit on during the later stages of pregnancy. During the early stages of labour it just helped to keep me comfortable whilst my husband sat behind me massaging my back. I found that sitting upright on it eased my contractions and was more comfortable than sitting on the bed. Bouncing on the ball helped me to be more comfortable right up until the later stages of labour. I'd definitely recommend it."

Marie Prime, New Mum

Labour, Birth, and Your Ball

Birth ball tips:

- A birth ball should be large enough that your hips are slightly higher than your knees when sitting on it.

- Always buy an anti-burst ball for pregnancy. These go down slowly if punctured and won't burst like a balloon. A non anti-burst ball may save you a little money, but it's just not worth the risk.

- Take your ball with you to the maternity unit or birthing centre. That way you know you'll have one during your labour, and it's hygienically clean.

- Get your partner to clean the ball with an anti-bacterial solution before bringing it home from hospital. It will only take a few minutes, and give you peace of mind.

- Sitting on the ball can help with the discomfort from Hemorrhoids during pregnancy, and also be soothing straight after the birth when sitting can be painful.

- Sitting on the ball can also be helpful in relieving the pain of Symphasis Pubis Dysfunction (SPD).

- Spending time on the ball during late pregnancy should help baby get in the right position for birth, giving you an easier and shorter labour.

- Your centre of gravity shifts as your pregnancy progresses. This can play havoc with your balance, so when you first sit on the ball, hold on with your hands to aid stability. Placing your feet wider apart will also give you a more stable base until your balance improves.

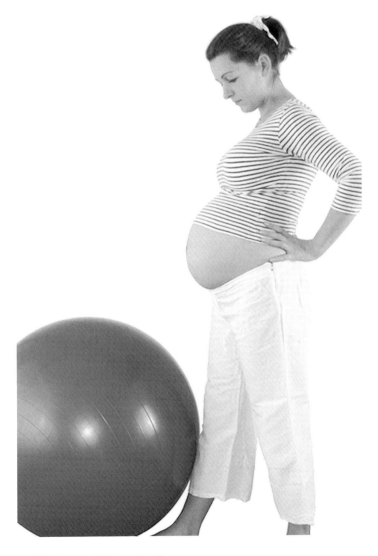

Labour, Birth, and Your Ball

7

Introduction to Postnatal Exercise

"I used a birthing ball throughout my pregnancy as I suffered from SPD and found the position of sitting on the ball and rocking really helped my pelvis. I also sat on a ball during early labour at home and throughout labour in the hospital - it was great for helping to concentrate my breathing, and balancing helped to take my mind off the contractions!! I have used it postnatally to regain my pre-pregnancy shape - and my husband has also used it to tone his tummy so it's useful for all the family!!!"

Gayle Waddell, New Mum, Cheshire.

Congratulations! You've had baby and are looking to get back some of your pre-pregnancy muscle tone. Well although you won't be entering into a full workout routine until after your six week check, (or longer after a c-section) there are still several things you can be doing right now.

Your Pelvic Floor

Your pelvic floor is made up of a sling of 3 muscles that connect the pubic bone at the front to the 'sitting bones' at the side and the tailbone at the back. This serves as a support structure for the contents of the abdomen and pelvis, including the bowel, uterus, and bladder. The extra weight of your growing baby made these muscles work even harder, and keeping them strong can help to prevent incontinence and prolapse. Hopefully you worked your Pelvic Floor throughout your pregnancy and the extra strength you gained helped you with the birth process. If you didn't then it's even more important that you start right now.

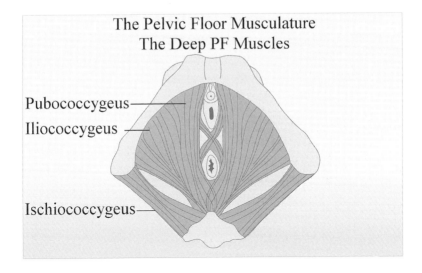

Learning to isolate and contract your pelvic floor muscles is easy. The next time you go for a wee just stop in mid flow and it will be these muscles doing the work. Aim to do it without clenching your buttocks or abdominals if possible as this brings in another set of muscles entirely. It is important that you don't actually do your pelvic floor exercises whilst urinating, as this could lead to problems like bladder infections.

"Your Pelvic Floor can be exercised as soon as you've given birth. This will help prevent or minimize embarrassing leaks when laughing, coughing, sneezing or lifting. As part of your 'core' it will also help you flatten your tummy sooner rather than later."

One good thing about pelvic floor exercises is that they can be done anywhere at any time, as only you know when you are doing them. Although you may have good intentions, the difficult thing is often remembering to do them. To help with this try to associate them with different activities such as ironing, cooking, driving, feeding baby, or when you're ready, having sex. After a while you'll find yourself doing them automatically when performing these activities. They should also be performed every day, several times if possible, and although at first you may find them difficult and tire easily, your strength and muscle control should increase rapidly. Here are some exercises for your pelvic floor.

1. Squeeze and hold

Squeeze/contract your pelvic floor muscles and hold for a count of 5 seconds. (Aim to build this to 10 seconds over a short period of time). Relax and rest for 10 seconds. Do 10 times, several times a day.

Introduction to Postnatal Exercise

2. Speed-ums

The pelvic floor is made up of 2 different types of muscle fibres. Some respond to quick contractions and some to slow. This exercise is for the 'quick' fibres.

Contract and lift the pelvic floor muscles as quickly and strongly as possible and let go. Gradually increase the speed of the contraction and the number of repetitions until the muscle tires. When the muscles are fatigued wait a few seconds to recover and start again. Aim to do these 10 times and repeat several times a day.

3. The lift

Try and visualise your midsection as a lift, then draw your pelvic floor upwards to the first floor and hold for 3 seconds. Breathing gently but without releasing the contraction, draw upwards to the second floor and hold for a further 3 seconds, then to the third floor for 3 seconds. Release and repeat several times a day.

Top Tip

"All these pelvic floor exercises can be performed sitting on your ball. This will engage your other core muscles even more, helping to tone your waistline and prevent injury."

Introduction to Postnatal Exercise

Exercising after a Caesarean Section

If you've had a c-section you will certainly have to wait longer before commencing a full exercise routine. However, there are still certain things you can do, and pelvic floor training is one of them. Even though you didn't have a normal vaginal delivery, your pelvic floor muscles will have had to work harder during your pregnancy to support the growing weight of your baby, so strengthening exercises are very important for you too.

Although heavy lifting is out of the question, it is important that you try to keep as active as possible. If you find walking comfortable, it can be a good low intensity way to burn extra calories. If you find yourself sitting or laying down much of the time, make sure you at least do some ankle pumping and rotation exercises to decrease the risk of a blood clot.

Some light core exercises, such as the ones on the accompanying DVD, can also be performed as can the pelvic tilts on the ball, but do check with your doctor or midwife first.

Other Waistline Exercises

It's important that after giving birth you don't rush back into a normal 'abdominal' routine. Your abdominal muscles will probably have separated to accommodate baby and will need to heal before you start performing the 'crunches' etc listed in this book. Some of the exercises however, are ok to do within the first few weeks. The pelvic tilts will work your abdominals without putting unnecessary strain on them, and in fact can help with the healing. The lateral pelvic tilts from the pregnancy exercise section can also be performed.

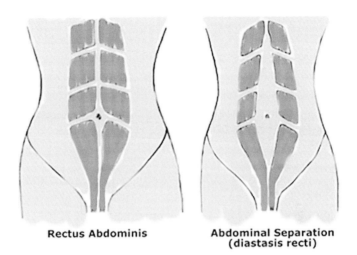

Rectus Abdominis

Abdominal Separation (diastasis recti)

After your muscles heal you can start working your waistline a little more intensely, but in some instances the abdominal separation can last longer then usual. This is called diastasis recti.

To check for diastasis recti lie on your back and raise your knees. Place your little finger in your navel and your other 3 fingers in a line toward your breastbone. Keeping your feet on the floor, lower your chin to your chest and slowly curl your head and shoulders off the floor as if you were performing a crunch. You may feel a gap appear so turn your fingers at a 90 degree angle to see how much separation you have. If the gap is more than two fingers wide you should definitely avoid regular abdominal exercises. Instead try this one.

Introduction to Postnatal Exercise

Lay flat on your back with your knees bent as above but fold/cross your hands over your stomach so they support your abdominals. Breathe in, and then as you slowly breathe out raise your head to your chest. Gently 'pull' your stomach muscles together and hold for a count of 2 then slowly lower your head to the floor. Repeat 10 times.

Training with Baby

You'll see that most of the postnatal exercises in this book include your baby, and working out with baby can be great for bonding and a whole lot of fun for both of you. It's also convenient because you don't have to worry about getting a babysitter every time you want to workout. However, don't worry if you'd rather train alone. All the exercises can be performed without baby too!

Top Tip

"If you start your programme when baby is only 6 weeks old, their weight gain over the next few months will serve as progressive resistance for your exercises. As baby gets heavier, you will get stronger which will help you with normal day to day activities."

Some of the guidelines associated with pregnancy exercise still apply during the postnatal period. It's still important that you do a thorough warm-up and cool-down before and after exercising. Stretches are always important at the end of a workout, but the relaxin hormone will still be present in your body (possibly for as long as you breastfeed), so stretching for maintenance only please and no ballistic or developmental stretching. If your joints become overextended while your connective tissue is still soft, after the hormones leave your body they will remain overextended. This can mean lax joints, causing pain, arthritis, and other problems.

For your postnatal ball routine:

- Always perform the hyperextensions, the shoulder rows, and the calf raises, and add two other exercises for each body section.

- Warm up and cool down properly

- Vary the exercises for all round development.

- Perform 2-3 sets of each exercise.

- Finish each workout with all the stretches.

- Aim to workout 3-4 times each week.

8

Postnatal Ball Routine

Quick Start Guide

This postnatal quick start guide is provided as a reminder for those of you who have read the book and understand the guidelines and the issues that may be associated with exercise during this period. Please do not start using this guide if you have not read this book or exercised with a ball before. We do not recommend including your baby in your routine unless you have achieved a good degree of core stability and are comfortable with your level of skill and balance whilst using your ball. Failing to heed this advice could be dangerous for you and your baby.

- Make sure you are wearing appropriate clothing, have fed or expressed, and have your water ready
- Choose the exercises you wish to do today
- If you're training with baby, make sure he/she's changed and happy
- Turn on your music and begin your warm up
- Exercise......and have fun bonding with baby!
- Cool down and don't forget to stretch (refer to Appendix 1)
- Well done! It's time for you both to relax until your next workout

Important stuff!

Always perform the hyperextensions, shoulder rows, and calf raises and keep hydrated!

Ball Press... tone your chest, shoulders and arms

- Upper Body Post Natal Exercises

1. Place feet shoulder width apart
2. Place ball between your hands and the wall, contract TVA and lean forward with your arms bent
3. Press against the ball until you are standing upright
4. Repeat 10-12 times

Postnatal Ball Routine

Baby Press... excellent for chest, shoulders and arms - Upper Body Post Natal Exercises

1. Lay on your back with your legs on the ball
2. Hold your baby on your chest
3. Breathe out, contract TVA, and press your baby upwards until your arms are straight
4. Lower baby to your chest
5. Repeat 12-15 times

Shoulder Row... upper back toner
- Upper Body Post Natal Exercises

1. Lay face down with your tummy on the ball and contract TVA
2. Bending your elbows, raise your arms up as if rowing a boat
3. At the top, squeeze your shoulder blades together
4. Return to start position
5. Repeat 12-15 times

Wall Squats... tone your thighs and buttocks
- Lower Body Post Natal Exercises

1. Stand with your feet shoulder width apart
2. Place your ball between the curve of your back and the wall and contract TVA
3. Bend your knees, squat down and return to the start position
4. Repeat 12-15 times
5. For added resistance hold baby close in front of you

Postnatal Ball Routine

Thigh Squeeze…for inner thigh and pelvic floor
- Lower Body Post Natal Exercises

1. Lie on your side and place ball between your ankles
2. Make sure your legs are straight
3. Contract your TVA and pelvic floor muscles and squeeze your ankles together
4. Hold for count of 5 and relax
5. Repeat 12-15 times

Postnatal Ball Routine

Ball Squat...tone those thighs and buttocks
- Lower Body Post Natal Exercises

1. Sit on your ball with your legs apart and your feet flat on floor. Contract TVA.
2. Without leaning forward, push up with your thighs to a standing position
3. Return to start position
4. Repeat 12-15 times
5. For added resistance hold baby close in front of you

Calf Raise… for toned lower legs
- Lower Body Post Natal Exercises

1. Sit on your ball and place your feet a few inches apart
2. Lay baby on your thighs and contract TVA
3. Raise your heels off the floor and contract your calf muscles
4. Return to the start position
5. Repeat 12-20 times

Pelvic Tilts... work your core
- Waistline Post Natal Exercises

1. Sit upright on the ball holding baby, or with arms crossed across your chest.
2. Contract TVA, and without moving your feet tilt your pelvis forward and upward.
3. Hold for a few seconds and return to start position.
4. Repeat 15-20 times

Postnatal Ball Routine

Ball Crunch... for a toned stomach
- Waistline Post Natal Exercises

1. Sit upright on the ball holding baby on your lap
2. Contract TVA and Roll out until your lower back is resting on the ball
3. Using your abdominal muscles, slowly curl your body upward until you feel a contraction in your abdominal muscles
4. Hold for a few seconds and return to the starting position
5. Repeat 15-20 times

Crunch... great for your abdominals
- Waistline Post Natal Exercises

1. Lie on the floor with your feet on your ball. Contract TVA
2. Exhale, and using your tummy muscles raise your shoulders off the floor
3. Hold for a second or two and return to the start position
4. Work up to 15-20 repetitions

Hyperextension… help strengthen your lower back - Waistline Post Natal Exercises

1. Lay face down with your tummy on the ball
2. Cross your arms in front of your body and contract TVA
3. Raise your upper body up until parallel to the floor
4. Slowly return to start position.
5. Repeat 12-15 times

Postnatal Ball Routine

Back, Shoulders and Chest Stretch
- Stretching Post Natal Exercises

1. Kneel in front of the ball
2. Roll the ball away from your body
3. With your head between your arms lean forward until you feel a stretch in your back, chest and shoulder muscles
4. Hold for 30 seconds and return to the start position

Postnatal Ball Routine

Chest and Bicep Stretch
- Stretching Post Natal Exercises

1. Sit on your ball
2. Walk your feet out until your upper back and shoulders are on the ball
3. Stretch your arms out and away from your body
4. Lower your hips slightly
5. Hold for 30 seconds and return to the start position
6. Everyone is different so find the position that works for you

Postnatal Ball Routine

Chest Stretch
- Stretching Post Natal Exercises

1. Kneel on the floor with the ball at your side
2. Bend forward at the waist and roll the ball out to the side until a stretch is felt in your chest
3. Hold for 30 seconds and repeat on the other side

Buttock Stretch
- Stretching Post Natal Exercises

1. Lie on your back with your right foot on the ball and your knee bent
2. Take your left foot and place the outside of the ankle on the right thigh, just below the knee
3. With your right heel, roll the ball towards your buttocks until you feel a stretch in your left buttock
4. Hold for 30 seconds and repeat on the other side

Postnatal Ball Routine

Hamstring Stretch
- Stretching Post Natal Exercises

1. Sit on the ball with your right leg out straight and your left leg bent
2. Place your hands on your left thigh
3. Lean forward until you feel a stretch in the back of your right thigh
4. Hold for 30 seconds and repeat on the other side

Hip Flexor Stretch
- Stretching Post Natal Exercises

1. Sit on the ball
2. Slide one leg behind the ball until it's straight
3. Maintaining good balance, lean back slightly until a stretch is felt in the top of the thigh
4. Hold for 30 seconds and repeat on the other side

Postnatal Ball Routine

9

Introduction to Advanced Exercises

"I can thoroughly recommend the use of an exercise/birth ball, I have been using mine for the last few months to strengthen my 'core' (something which I knew nothing about until I had my baby 10 months ago)! I've never had the most perfect body, but by using my trusty ball and taking my wonderful baby out for lots of walks, I'm actually starting to quite like my post-pregnancy body (something I never did pre-pregnancy)!!!

I'm finding myself feeling stronger and having lots more energy than I ever had. I simply bounce my way to fitness and my beautiful daughter finds mummy's bouncing pretty entertaining in the meantime! Now who can argue with the hearty chuckles of a loving child? Not me, that's for sure!

Ps: The ball has also helped alleviate a lower back problem I've had since I was a teenager! All hail the birth ball!!"

Yours bouncingly,

Keri Struth, New Mum

When is the postnatal period over?

That often depends on you. How fit you were before you got pregnant, how much you exercised during your pregnancy, what kind of birth you had, and how active you've been since will all play a part. Individual fitness and strength levels can vary dramatically from person to person, and the length of time the relaxin hormone stays in the body also varies from mother to mother. Some 'experts' are still quoting five months or less, others up to one year, and some believe that relaxin can stay in your body as long as you are breastfeeding. In reality, if you have no qualified fitness professional guiding you, you are probably the best person to judge whether you're ready to move on to the more advanced stretching and toning exercises outlined in this book. However, if you're not sure, always err on the side of caution.

When it comes to stretching, even if you are one of the new mums who doesn't feel 'loose' in the joints, we still recommend that you wait at least 20 weeks after the birth before you do anything more than normal maintenance stretching. Even if you were a regular exerciser, runner, or athlete before your pregnancy and you are itching to get back to something more intense like PNF stretching, we'd advise you not to succumb to temptation because any connective tissue damage you do now could be permanent.

By now you should be feeling fitter and seeing great results from the previous exercises. You'll also be confident exercising with the ball and looking for new challenges. If that's the case then you're ready to move on.

Introduction to Advanced Exercises

Advanced ball routine tips

- Choose 3 exercises from each section and vary them each workout to achieve good all round development.

- Warm up and cool down properly

- Increase the intensity, and look for improvement each week

- Try to workout 3-4 times per week

- Finish your workout by performing all the stretches

- Make sure you keep hydrated. The harder you work out the more fluid you will need to replace.

10

Advanced Ball Routine

Quick Start Guide

This advanced quick start guide is provided as a reminder for those of you who have already read the book and understand the information therein. Please do not start using this guide if you have not read this book or exercised with a ball before. Under no account should this routine be performed when pregnant or during the postnatal period as it contains a number of exercises that are unsuitable for this period. Failure to heed this advice could be dangerous for you and your baby!

- Pregnancy & Postnatal implications are over. Now you can GO FOR IT!
- Choose 3 exercises each for upper body, lower body and waistline
- Turn on the music and begin your warm up
- Train hard, and increase the intensity for quicker results
- Cool down and stretch your muscles (refer to Appendix 1)
- Well done! Now relax......you deserve it

Important stuff

- Choose 3 exercises from each section
- Vary the exercises each time for all round development
- Keep hydrated when exercising
- Aim to improve your strength and flexibility every week
- Train intensely for quick results

Advanced Ball Routine

Press Up... work your chest and arms
- Upper Body Advanced Exercises

1. Roll onto the ball walking hands forward until your upper legs are on the ball
2. Keep head and body aligned. Don't look up
3. Contract TVA and lower your body until your elbows reach a 90 degree angle
4. Push back to start position and repeat 12 times

Dumbell Flyes... great chest toning exercise
- Upper Body Advanced Exercises

1. Holding two hand weights sit on the ball and roll out until your upper back is resting on the ball
2. Keeping your body straight, press the weights up above your eyes
3. With elbows bent, lower the weights out to your side until a slight stretch is felt in your chest muscles
4. In the same arc, return to the start position
5. Perform 12-15 times.

Dumbell Chest Press...for chest toning
- Upper Body Advanced Exercises

1. Holding two hand weights sit on the ball and roll out until your upper back is resting on the ball
2. Keeping your body straight, contract TVA and press the weights up above your eyes.
3. Lower the weights until your elbows are at a 90 degree angle
4. Press back to the start position, and repeat 12-15 times

Reverse Flyes... tone and strengthen your upper back - Upper Body Advanced Exercises

1. Lay face down with hips and tummy on the ball. Contract TVA
2. With elbows at 90 degrees raise arms up and out to the sides bringing shoulder blades together
3. Lower to start position and repeat 12 times
4. To increase difficulty use hand weights

Advanced Ball Routine

Shoulder Press... toned shoulders
- Upper Body Advanced Exercises

1. Sit on the ball with feet firmly on the floor, Contract TVA
2. Raise hand weights to shoulder height, and with elbows at 90 degrees press weights above head
3. Lower slowly to start position (90 degrees) and repeat 12 times

Advanced Ball Routine

Bicep Curl... stronger and toned arms
- Upper Body Advanced Exercises

1. Sit on the ball with hand weights at arms length beside you
2. Contract TVA and with elbows pointing straight down, curl the weights to your shoulders
3. Lower slowly to start position and repeat 12 times

Arm Leg Extension… for upper back, balance and core - Upper Body Advanced Exercises

1. Kneel in front of the ball, place your chest on the ball and hands on the floor in front of you
2. Contract your TVA and slowly lift your left arm and right leg simultaneously
3. When your arm and leg are parallel to the floor, hold for 5 seconds and return to start position
4. Change to opposite side and repeat 12 times on each

Wall Squat... firm legs and buttocks
- Lower Body Advanced Exercises

1. Stand with feet shoulder width apart
2. Place ball between the curve of your back and the wall, contract TVA
3. Bend your knees, squat down to 90 degrees and return to start position
4. Repeat 12-15 times

Advanced Ball Routine

Inner Thigh Squeeze...toned inner thighs
- Lower Body Advanced Exercises

1. Lie on your back with knees slightly bent and arms on floor
2. Place ball between lower legs, contract TVA, and slowly squeezing legs together, raise hips off the floor
3. When body is completely straight, hold for a few seconds and slowly return to start position
4. Repeat 12 times

Leg Curl... great legs
- Lower Body Advanced Exercises

1. Lie face up on floor with calves and feet on ball and hands on floor
2. Contract TVA, lift buttocks off floor and pull the ball toward you using your legs
3. Keeping TVA contracted and body straight, continue until knees are bent to 90 degrees
4. Slowly push ball away again until legs are nearly straight, and repeat 12 times

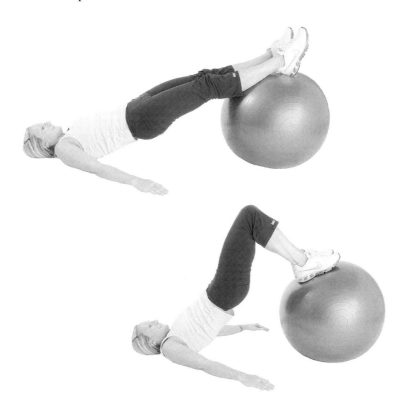

Advanced Ball Routine

Reverse Bridge... work your legs, buttocks and core - Lower Body Advanced Exercises

1. Lay on your back with calves on the ball and arms out to your sides
2. With feet slightly apart, contract TVA and lift your buttocks off the floor until your body is straight
3. Hold for 5 seconds and return to start position.
4. Repeat 12 times. For added stability place your feet wider apart

Advanced Ball Routine

Calf Raise...toned calves
- Lower Body Advanced Exercises

1. Stand upright with ball at chest height between you and the wall
2. Step slightly away from the wall and lean into ball
3. Contract TVA, and holding sides of ball, rise up onto toes
4. Squeeze calf muscles, return to the start position, and repeat 15 times

Abdominal Crunch... for a firmer stomach
- Waistline Advanced Exercises

1. Sit on the ball and roll out until lower back is on ball
2. Place hands loosely on head (no pressure on neck) and contract TVA
3. Slowly curl your upper body toward your pelvis and contract abdominal muscles
4. Hold for a few seconds, return to start position and repeat 12-15 times

Crunch with Twist...work your obliques
- Waistline Advanced Exercises

1. Sit on the ball and roll out until lower back is on ball
2. Place hands loosely on head (no pressure on neck) and contract TVA
3. Slowly curl your upper body toward your pelvis whilst rotating torso to the left
4. Return to start position and repeat on other side. Repeat 12-15 times

Roll Out… excellent for firm abs
- Waistline Advanced Exercises

1. Kneel in front of ball with knees on a mat or folded towel and contract TVA
2. With elbows slightly bent, place hands on ball and roll ball forward
3. Hold abdominal contraction for 5 seconds and roll ball back towards you
4. Repeat 12-15 times

Hyperextension... works your lower back
- Waistline Advanced Exercises

1. Lay face down with your tummy on the ball
2. Cross your arms in front of your body and contract TVA
3. Using your lower back muscles, raise upper body until parallel to the floor
4. Slowly return to start position and repeat 12-15 times

The Plank… tough on the abs
- Waistline Advanced Exercises

1. Kneel in front of the ball with fists clenched and forearms on ball
2. Contract TVA and straighten your legs until your body is straight with a 90 degree angle at the elbow
3. Hold for 5-10 seconds and slowly return to the start position
4. Repeat 12-15 times

Advanced Ball Routine

Side Stretch
- Stretching Advanced Exercises

1. Kneel next to the ball and lean over it lowering your bottom arm to the floor
2. Straightening your top leg, stretch your body over the ball until you feel a stretch in the muscles down your side
3. Return to the start position and perform 15 repetitions. Repeat on other side

Advanced Ball Routine

Hip Flexor Stretch
- Stretching Advanced Exercises

1. Sit on the ball and slide one leg behind ball until straight
2. Maintaining your balance lean back slightly until a stretch is felt at the top of your thigh
3. Hold for 30 seconds and repeat on other side
4. If maintaining balance is a problem hold on to a wall or table

Hamstring Stretch
- Stretching Advanced Exercises

1. Sit on the ball with your right leg out straight and your left leg bent
2. Place your hands on your left thigh
3. Lean forward until you feel a stretch in the back of your right thigh
4. Hold for 30 seconds and repeat on the other side

Quad Stretch
- Stretching Advanced Exercises

1. Hold on to a wall or chair and place your outside foot/shin on the ball
2. Bend your inside knee slightly while rolling ball backwards with outside leg
3. When a stretch is felt in your quadriceps, hold for 30 seconds and return to start position

Hip/Buttock Stretch
- Stretching Advanced Exercises

1. Lie on your back with your right foot on the ball and your knee bent
2. Take your left foot and place the outside of the ankle on the right thigh, just below the knee
3. With your right heel, roll the ball towards your buttocks until you feel a stretch in your left buttock
4. Hold for 30 seconds and repeat on the other side

Calf Stretch
- Stretching Advanced Exercises

1. Kneel in front of the ball and lean forward so your body and arms are over the ball
2. Push one leg out straight behind you so your toe is on the floor and heel in the air
3. Roll your body back slightly and push your heel away from your body
4. When a stretch is felt in calf, hold for 30 seconds and return to start position

Advanced Ball Routine

Chest Stretch
- Stretching Advanced Exercises

1. Kneel on the floor with the ball at your side
2. Bend forward at the waist and roll the ball out to the side until a stretch is felt in your chest
3. Hold for 30 seconds and repeat on the other side

Advanced Ball Routine

11

8 Super Secrets for getting your pre-pregnancy figure back...........Fast!

So it's a few months after the birth and baby's growing up fast. You've been good and have eaten reasonably well, exercised when you can, and yet you still look and feel 'flabby' around your waistline and bum.

What's the best way to conquer this problem?

Well please don't consider going back to any of the diet plans you may have used before your pregnancy, because most 'diets' leave you feeling weak, hungry, and stressed. Also, for a number of reasons, when you finish them you'll usually put any weight you lost straight back on and sometimes even more.

8 Simple Rules:

There are 8 simple rules for healthy and lasting weight loss, and when you get used to making them a regular part of your daily routine, you'll have the key to a happy and healthy life.

Rule 1: Visualise

Get out of the mindset that it'll be difficult or that it can't be done, because negative thinking will defeat you from the start. If you can't see where you're going you'll never get there, so try to get in shape in your mind before you actually do it in person. Visualise how you'd like to look in a few months time. Close your eyes and imagine you're there already. Think about what it will be like, and feel like, when you look the way you want to look. Think of the wonderful clothes you will wear, and the admiring and envious glances you'll get from those around you. If you do this consistently twice a day you'll programme your subconscious mind into believing you look that way already, and you'll get there before you know it. It may sound far fetched, but this type of visualisation is performed daily by successful people worldwide, whether they are Olympic athletes or business leaders.

Rule 2: Keep Active

Although you can start exercising your pelvic floor muscles as soon as you have given birth (and you should) if there are no medical reasons not to, a full exercise program should not be undertaken until a few weeks after the birth. When you've recovered and are getting into a routine then it's important to your future fat loss goals that you keep active. Many of us live an increasingly sedentary lifestyle these days and that's leading to a whole host of health problems, obesity being just one of them.

One great way to start getting active is to walk with baby. You can start walking quite soon after childbirth and it's a great way to burn calories. Taking your baby out in the buggy for a walk will get them off to sleep and start you on the road to weight loss. You will need to get your heart rate up though, so it's important that you don't just saunter. After the first few days vary the pace. Go uphill, downhill, and push the buggy on grass so you get a good workout. Walk for at least 20-30 minutes so you give your body a chance to burn fat. Going with a friend makes it a social thing and the time will pass more quickly. If you have no one to go with join a stroller group. These have been happening in the US for years and are finally making it big over here.

But apart from the obvious calorie burning benefits, what other good reasons are there to exercise? Well it's common knowledge that exercise produces as many mental benefits as physical benefits. There's just something about exercise that makes us feel better. This is believed to be because exercise releases endorphins into the bloodstream which have an analgesic effect on the body resulting in a state of euphoria. Other reasons why exercise makes us feel better can include the sense of achievement we feel after actually motivating ourselves to complete a workout or run, and also the fact that exercise can simply provide a distraction from the everyday stresses of life.

Numerous other benefits to be had from regular exercise include increased energy levels (and you'll certainly benefit from that), reduced anxiety and stress, increased muscular endurance, improved posture, less chance of Post Natal Depression, and the list goes on. All in all it's very easy to see why it's so important to incorporate exercise in to our daily routines. Yes it may be hard at first, but if you persevere it will become a habit and one you won't want to give up.

Rule 3: Avoid processed foods

Processed foods, and there are more and more available these days, are a sure-fire way of gaining fat, mainly because of their synthetic, sugar and salt laden make-up. Most processed foods are pretty devoid of vitamins and minerals and are loaded with calories and toxins which end up buried in your fatty tissues. The nature of processed foods also means you'll retain a whole lot of water, making you not only gain weight but look soft and bloated too. Lovely!

Healthy Eating Tips:

- Eat small, frequent meals (5-6 per day) rather than one or two large ones, and eat them as soon as you are hungry. Waiting until you are famished means your blood glucose levels have plummeted and when you do eat you'll overdo it. Eating smaller meals provides 'metabolic bursts' and each meal will raise your metabolic rate. This is especially true if protein is included and this has the added benefit of keeping your hunger at bay for longer.

- Eat a healthy and nutritious diet with lots of fresh fruit and vegetables. We have put the emphasis on 'fresh' here although these days frozen can be just as good. Another good source is from your local farm shop or farmers market if possible to enjoy produce at its best and most nutritious. If you are concerned about not getting the sufficient amount of vitamins and minerals from your food then use a high quality vitamin/mineral supplement.

- Don't skip meals. This will lower your metabolic rate during the day, and in turn cause you to snack on empty calories.

- Protein and carbohydrate has 4 calories per gram, and fat has 9 calories per gram so do the maths! Eat a diet that is lower in fat but don't cut it out completely as your body needs it to function properly. Less than 30% of your calories should be from fat, and less than 10% from saturated fat. These are usually listed individually on the food labels.

- Avoid Starchy Carbohydrates whenever you can. If you eat starchy carbohydrates on their own, or combined with sweet and sugary carbohydrates, it will raise your insulin to an extremely high level which in turn commands your body to store fat. Mixing your carbs with protein reduces the effect and amount of the insulin boost, keeping your fat loss on track.

Top Tip

"Breastfeeding mums should not concentrate on weight loss, as they need to consume up to an extra 500 calories per day."

Rule 4: Keep Hydrated

Despite some recent 'studies' stating we don't need as much water as we thought, when it comes to losing weight the importance of proper hydration cannot be emphasised enough. Your body will give you false food cravings when you are thirsty, causing you to think you're hungry and consume extra calories unnecessarily. Drinking plenty of water also speeds up the digestion process allowing food to pass quickly and easily through your system. On the other hand, if you let yourself get dehydrated it means undigested food will stay in your stomach much longer, going putrid, and poisoning your system.

Tips to keep hydrated.

- Drink at least 8 glasses of water per day, and don't wait until you are thirsty as by this time it's too late, you are already dehydrated! You need water to replenish lost fluids, and the more active you are, the more you need.

- Many times when you feel hungry you are actually thirsty. So, take a nice cool zero calorie drink instead of eating food you don't actually need, and please don't substitute caffeine, fizzy drinks, or alcohol for water. These are diuretics that will actually cause you to lose water through increased urination.

- We all know that exercise combined with proper nutrition is the best way to lose weight and keep it off, but when you exercise you will lose more fluids and therefore will need to drink more to avoid dehydration. Once you do start exercising, drink water throughout your workouts. Keep a bottle with you and take frequent water breaks.

- Your body loses water while you sleep so it's a good idea to start and end your day with water. If you drink some before you go to bed and again when you wake up, it will help to keep you hydrated

Rule 5: Sleep Well

We know that's not always easy when you have a new baby in the house, but your body restores itself during sleep. Tissue grows and repairs itself and your immune system becomes stronger. For years we have thought that sleeping too much would contribute to weight gain but it seems the opposite is true. Scientists have recently reached the conclusion that it's too little sleep that makes you fat! This is because sleep deprivation decreases the levels of a hormone that makes you feel full (leptin) and increases the levels of an appetite stimulating hormone (ghrelin). The effects of this can lead to overeating and weight gain and are part of the reason that new parents are susceptible to piling on the pounds. Not getting enough sleep also puts undue stress on the body, releasing the stress hormone cortisol and breaking down lean muscle tissue

Tips for a good nights sleep.

- Don't eat right before bed, but eat a good dinner earlier in the evening so you don't feel hungry when you go to bed.

- Exercise will help you sleep and lose weight, but don't exercise right before bed as it stimulates your metabolism and can prevent you sleeping.

- Avoid caffeine, alcohol, and cigarettes totally if possible, but certainly in the evenings.

- Make your bedroom as dark as possible and a comfortable place to be.

- If your little one isn't yet going through the night, try and nap with them during the day. It's far more important than daytime TV!

- Do your best to keep to a bedtime routine. Bath, book, hot chocolate, or whatever. It works for baby and it can work for you too.

Rule 6: Avoid Microwave Ovens when possible

Have you ever wondered why you feel hungry so soon after microwave 'TV Dinners'? Have you ever watched the 'food programmes' on TV and seen the poor health of people who live mainly on 'microwave meals'? Well maybe it's because during the heating process microwaves vibrate the molecules of your food so fast that they actually change their structure, meaning that when you eat microwave food, your body has no idea about how to cope with it, let alone extract nutrition from it. This has the result of giving you a surplus of non-nutritional calories which can lead to weight gain.

If you'd like to read a scientific version, the article *'In Comparative Study of Food Prepared Conventionally and in the Microwave Oven'*, published by **Raum & Zelt in 1992,** states

"A basic hypothesis of natural medicine states that the introduction into the human body of molecules and energies, to which it is not accustomed, is much more likely to cause harm than good. Microwave food contains both molecules and energies not present in food cooked in the way humans have been cooking food since the discovery of fire. Microwave energy from the sun and other stars is direct current based. Artificially produced microwaves, including those in ovens, are produced from alternating current and force a billion or more polarity reversals per second in every food molecule they hit. Production of unnatural molecules is inevitable. Naturally occurring amino acids have been observed to undergo isomeric changes (changes in shape morphing) as well as transformation into toxic forms, under the impact of microwaves produced in ovens."

It's your choice

Of course there are other articles available stating that microwaves are safe, so as always the choice is yours? However, it stands to reason that if food is structurally altered then the nutritional value will be negated. Of course microwaves are convenient, and these days everyone's time seems to be at a premium, so, like most things, moderation would seem to be the order of the day.

8 Super Secrets

Rule 7: Cut down on alcohol

We are not trying to spoil all your fun here, but there are 7 calories in a gram of alcohol, and it's pretty much pure sugar. This means it's packed full of calories that add nothing to the function of your body. It'll also make you retain water so you look bloated and swollen.

Rule 8: Set goals

Please remember that Rome wasn't built in a day. It's a bit of a cliché to say 'it took you nine months to get out of shape, so it'll take you nine to get back' but it's probably quite realistic. Remember your body has 'climbed a mountain' during your pregnancy and needs time to heal inside and out. So many people will quit an exercise program or eating plan because of unrealistic expectations. It's important that you set short and long term goals, so take a good look at yourself and decide where you want to be in 3 weeks, 3 months, 6 months, and 1 year and set your goals accordingly. Don't be worried about rewarding yourself when you reach your short term goals either. For example if chocolate is your thing, it will be much easier to stop eating it for a while if you know it's not banished completely, and you can reward yourself with some when you hit a short term goal. This way you are much more likely to stay on track and get the desired results. You may want to use the **SMART** acronym for goal setting.

Specific
Measurable
Attainable
Realistic
Timely

Specific

Make sure your long term goal is not just a general 'I want to lose weight'. It has to be more specific such as 'I want to lose 14 lbs'. Then you should write down what you are going to do to achieve it, why it is important at this time, (if you don't feel it's important enough you won't get it done), and how you are going to get it done.

Measurable

This is where your short term goals come in. You need to be able to measure along the way to check your progress, and you need to do it regularly to keep you on track. This is how programs such as 'Slimming World' and 'Weight Watchers' get great results. The weekly weigh in keeps you focused, and when you experience the exhilaration of achievement it will spur you on to the continued effort required to reach your goals.

Attainable

If a goal is too far out of reach you will not seriously commit to doing it no matter how good your original intentions were. A goal will need to stretch you slightly, so you feel you can do it but it will need a commitment from you to achieve it. If you want to lose 20lbs don't set a goal to do it in a week because it'll never happen. If you set a goal of 2lbs per week however, it will be attainable and will spur you on to do the next 2lbs and so on. It's the feeling of success that keeps you motivated.

Realistic

This means do-able, not easy. You must set the bar high enough for a satisfying achievement. Setting it too low sends the message that you aren't very capable, but too high may set you up for failure.

Timely

Start now, and set a time frame for your goal. Not setting a time frame is too vague and does not give you a clear target to work towards. If you feel you can start at any time it will tend not to happen. You need urgency to make you take the appropriate action NOW.

The **SMART** way of goal setting will help you to plan and therefore to achieve the desired results from your exercise and nutrition program.

There are plenty of gimmicks on the weight loss market, and they sell because people are looking for instant gratification or an easy option. Lasting results however, come from developing good habits and doing them day in day out, not for a month now and again. The 8 simple rules described above are the habits that will give you the lasting results you want. Do all you can to live by these rules and you'll never again have to go on a diet. You'll look and feel fantastic, you'll have all the energy you'll ever need to play with and look after your children, and you'll be the envy of all your friends.

Now you have the 'the 8 secrets' the rest is up to you.

Appendix 1

Warm up, Cool Down, and Stretching

Correctly warming up before exercise is extremely important, especially during pregnancy and the postnatal period. During pregnancy your circulatory system has been affected meaning a slower, gradual approach to your warm up is necessary to allow for adjustments in blood volume. Moving through your warm up too quickly could result in a rise in blood pressure and breathlessness.

The idea of a warm up is to prepare your body for exercise, and warming up properly is recognised as key for preventing injury. By warming up properly you will not only be increasing the supply of oxygen and nutrients to your muscles making them more supple and ready for exercise and stretching, but your heart and mind will also be preparing themselves for an increase in activity.

Make sure you pay particular attention to your posture and perform all warm up movements slowly, in a controlled fashion, and within a normal range of movement.

Your warm up should consist of 10 minutes of light, low intensity exercise.

Example warm up

- Begin your warm up by walking on the spot with good posture and your arms at your sides. (2 min)

- Breathe continuously, and as you walk, start to make gentle circles with your head to warm up the muscles in your neck. (1 min)
- Roll your shoulders backward and forward to warm up the muscles in your shoulders and upper body. (1 min)
- Raise your arms slowly out to shoulder height and return to your sides several times. (1 min)
- Start to lift your knees slightly higher now maintaining good posture and pump your arms slowly and firmly in a curling movement (palms up) to warm up the muscles in your arms. (1 min)
- Raise your arms out to your sides again and perform controlled circular movements with your hands. (1 min)
- Repeat the shoulder rolling and arm curling movements one more time. (2 mins)
- Holding onto a chair or table for support, perform some shallow (half) squats or knee bends. (1 min)

After performing this type of warm up routine for 10 minutes you should have a light sweat and be ready for your exercise routine.

Cooling Down

Cooling down after exercise is also important as it allows your heart rate and breathing to return to normal gradually. This can help to prevent blood pooling and post exercise hypotension (low blood pressure). To cool down repeat the warm up procedure, until you feel your heart rate and breathing have returned to normal.

Stretching

Stretching is an integral part of your routine, and is best integrated into, or performed after the cool down when your muscles are still warm. This is when there is less chance of injury. Stretching will relax your muscles and help them to return to their normal length.

Warm Up, Cool Down and Stretching Guidelines

- Always maintain good posture
- Always warm up and cool down gradually
- Always avoid sudden changes of direction
- Always avoid extended range of movement
- Always rise and change direction slowly
- Always move slowly and gently
- In later pregnancy hold onto something for support
- Never over stretch as it could lead to injury

If you feel pain, stop immediately!

Appendix 2

Training Notes

Appendices

Training Notes

Training Notes

Training Notes

Training Notes

Training Notes

Training Notes

Index

A

abdominal crunch 94
abdominal separation 57
advanced balance 37
alcohol 114
anaemia 13
anti-burst 50
arm-leg extension 88
arrhythymia 13

B

baby press 62
back 72
back pain 11,44
ball crunch 69
ball squat 66
bicep curl 24,87
bicep stretch 73
buttock stretch 75

C

c-section 11,56
calf pain 14
calf raises 30,67,93
calf stretches 41,43,72,73,74,105
cat stretch 42
carbohydrates 109,110
chest pain 14

cool down 18,59,80,117,118
core muscles 46
crunch 70,95

D

developmental stretching
diastasis recti 57
dumbell chest press 84
dumbell flyes 83
DVD 56
DVT 14
dyna band curls 25

E

endorphins 108

F

fat 109,110
flabby 106

G

gestational diabetes 11
ghrehin 112
glute 104

H

hamstring stretch 39,76,101
headache 14
heart disease 13
hip flexor stretch 38,77,100
hip/glute stretch 103
hormone relaxin 17
hyperextension 71,97
hypertension 11
hyperthyroidism 14

I

incline dumbell flyes 21
incline dumbell press 22
incontinence 53
inner thigh squeeze 90

L

lateral raise 27
lateral pelvic 33
lateral stretch 40
leg cramps 11
leg curl 91
leptin 112

Index

M

metabolic bursts 109

O

obesity 13

P

pelvic floor 44,45,53,55,107
pelvic tilts 31,56,68
plank 98
PND 108
PNF 79
postnatal 79
preeclampsia 13
protein 109
preterm labour 14
press up 23,82
processed food 108
protein 109

Q

quad stretch 102

S

seated balance 34
shoulders 72
shoulder press 86
shoulder stretch 99
shoulder row 63
side stretch 99

sit backs 32
sleep 111
split squat 29
SPD 50
standing balance 36
stretching 119
squat 28

T

thigh squeeze 65
tricep extension 26
TVA 15,16

V

vaginal bleeding 14

W

waistline 106
wall press 61
wall squat 64,89
warm up 18,59,80, 117
water 110,111
weight loss 106